# Spare

## 60 Skeletal Scenes
## for Acting and Directing

**DIANE TIMMERMAN**

HEINEMANN
Portsmouth, NH

**Heinemann**
361 Hanover Street
Portsmouth, NH 03801–3912
www.heinemanndrama.com

*Offices and agents throughout the world*

© 2005 by Diane Timmerman

**Library of Congress Cataloging-in-Publication Data**
Timmerman, Diane.
   Spare scenes : 60 skeletal scenes for acting and directing / Diane Timmerman.
      p. cm.
   Includes bibliographical references.
   ISBN 0-325-00707-1 (alk.paper)
   1. Acting.  2. Theater—Production and direction.  I. Title.

PN2080.T56 2005
812'.6—dc22                                    2004019449

Editor: Lisa A. Barnett
Production: Vicki Kasabian
Cover design: Night & Day Design
Author photograph: Ed Moss
Typesetter: Tom Allen, Pear Graphic Design
Manufacturing: Louise Richardson

Printed in the United States of America on acid-free paper
T & C Digital

# Contents

# Acknowledgments

Every acting and directing teacher I know steals like a thief and I am no exception. I believe the unwritten agreement is that as long as you acknowledge what has come before you are free to use it. At least, I hope that's the agreement. In any case, I'd like to thank my teachers Howard Jensen, Dale McFadden, and Bruce Burgun at Indiana University and, even more years ago, Kyle Donnelly and Eileen Vorbach at the Actors' Center in Chicago. The Actors' Center work and that of Bruce was influenced by Edward-Kaye Martin and the great Sanford Meisner. I would also like to thank Robert Cohen for originating the idea of contentless scenes in his book, *Acting Power*.

I thank Dan Barden for providing me with abundant examples of clean, powerful writing, David Mold for lending his editorial insight, and my parents for teaching me about unconditional generosity. Thanks, too, to Owen Schaub, John Green, and Peter Alexander for making coming to work so much fun.

I also thank Kristin Linklater, Andrea Haring, Trudie Kessler, Christine Adaire, Louis Colaianni, and all of my 2003 Designated Linklater voice instructor buddies for teaching me that speaking the truth is one of life's beautiful experiences.

For the last decade my students at Butler University have been my teachers. They have taught me how to teach. Over the years, they have created such life from spare words the likes I have never seen. The words on these pages are no doubt part of the indelible memory their performances have etched on my heart.

Everyone in theatre knows that part of the journey is getting back to the freedom of childhood. Every parent knows the potency of a child's words, the power of a few syllables screamed or cried or cooed or whispered. The urgency, purity, abandon, and passion of my children, Charis, Barek, and Asher, energize each word I write, each role I act, each play I direct. Perhaps even more amazing is the way my husband, Steve Webb, manages to retain the wildness of childhood while doing all the adult things he does. My family teaches me every day and for that I am profoundly grateful.

# Introduction

Why write a book of scenes about nothing—scenes that have no specific place, content, or characters? I needed these open scenes—desperately—for class. How do you teach that acting is about relationships, behavior, and interactions between people? How do you teach that, although language is of paramount importance, in contemporary theatre what is happening underneath and inside and alongside the lines is what makes the performance? How do you unchain actors from the notion that learning the lines is the big deal when you know the big deal is something much deeper? How do you coax sensuality, surprise, delight, anguish, cruelty, and passion out of actors who sometimes can't access those feelings when fettered with circumstance-laden words on a page that set up preconceived notions of how it all "should be"?

For me, I take away the words. Starting in silence, actors create relationships. Slowly, words are added through improvisation. Ultimately scripted dialogue is used, but when that day comes, it helps if those words are spare. Minimalist language forces actors to make specific decisions about character, relationship, and action because these ideas are not given in the text. The interaction between actors becomes the focal point because the words they are saying are seemingly insignificant. Open scenes underscore the importance of making strong emotional, physical, and vocal choices, and living in the moment with a scene partner.

Other things come later, of course. The visceral and intellectual importance of heightened language—even in contemporary drama—needs to be fully explored. This exploration climaxes with Shakespeare, a theatre of language, where, in fact, character, relationship, and action reside in the words. Undeniably, text is a vital component of most types of theatre. But I have found it useful to step back from language, allowing other aspects of performance to rise to prominence. Because the words of the scenes in this book have relatively little value in and of themselves, the relationships created by the actors and the spontaneous moments between them take the focus. With small words and huge choices, an actor can discover what it means to act.

How then to use these scenes? The simple answer is: however you like! They can be used for a variety of acting and directing exercises and performances that demonstrate giving and receiving action, creating bold acting choices, developing the physical life of a character, creating relationships, environments, tone, and emphasis. There are countless ways to incorporate *Spare Scenes* into the classroom, and many teachers will already know how they wish to utilize the scenes. Some teachers may want to assign several pairs in a class the same scene, with each pair creating different relationships, circumstances, and environments that evolve over the course of several weeks. Others may want to use the scenes for cold readings in order to strengthen the actors' ability to make bold relationship and action choices in the moment. Still others may want to use these scenes as a tool to support work on scenes from full-length plays by having the actors use the skeletal dialogue for improv-like scenes that explore and develop the characters, relationships, and given circumstances of the play. The scenes might also be used in beginning voice and speech classes, where students are developing the ability to speak with their own voice in connection to a text. As the students' voices develop in range and power, the circumstances of the scenes can be heightened in order to serve as vehicles for expanding vocal capabilities.

A word about the language of *Spare Scenes:* I have purposely pared down punctuation to a minimum, with commas, question marks, and ellipses added only when absolutely necessary and exclamation points completely eschewed. Because the point of these scenes is to allow for maximum interpretation, it is understood—encouraged, even—that in performance these scenes will take on whatever punctuation the circumstances and relationship dictate, regardless of what appears or does not appear on the page. The same holds true for pacing: I have not included any pauses in the text, but if and when a moment calls for a pause or silence, the actors should feel free to take the time they need. The scenes can be played at a rapid-fire pace, but it is also valuable to slow them down, either in their entirety or for a section. The actors can experiment with allowing the scenes to breathe, speaking only when they have a genuine impulse to communicate. It is also worth noting that although conflict is inherent in most of the scenes, each can also be played with positive objectives and circumstances.

In order to help teachers get the most out of these scenes, I have provided acting and directing exercises on the following pages. These exercises can serve as a supplement to other acting textbooks and classroom activities. The exercises are as skeletally designed as the scenes themselves, and teachers should feel free to improvise with them in whatever way they find most useful.

# Exercises for the Acting Classroom

Each of the steps below will take from 20 minutes to several class sessions to accomplish, depending upon the size of the group. Between steps, it can be helpful to pause for feedback from the actors and the class audience about what they observed in each improvisation.

Steps 1 to 3 provide one way to create relationships, characters, and situations that can then be applied to a *Spare Scene*. (Other ideas for approaching the scenes are listed after Step 7.)

### STEP #1: CREATING A RELATIONSHIP FOR USE IN A *SPARE SCENE*

- Acting partners choose a relationship

    ◦ Pick a relationship with a lot at stake: couples, best friends, roommates, siblings, or, if there is age diversity in the class, parent/child.

- Acting partners build the relationship

    ◦ Off on their own, partners discuss the facts of their relationship: how long they have known each other and how they met if they are not family, what their family is like if they are related.

    ◦ Partners converse, making it up as they go: what was the best time of their life together, what was the worst time they ever shared, and what do they do on a typical day spent together.

### STEP #2: DEVELOPING THE RELATIONSHIP THROUGH IMPROVISATION

- Select a location for the improvisations

    ◦ The home of one or both of the characters works well.

- Play a silent improv of a typical day in the life of the two characters

    o One person is outside the agreed-upon location for the improv and one is already at the location. Nothing is up, it's just another day, and the outside person is arriving where the other is.

    o Actors should forgo miming or mouthing language and simply be in the space with one another, relating silently and physically as they wish. Nothing much needs to happen except for attention to one another and some eye contact.

- Play a silent improv that involves an action or objective

    o One actor goes offstage to brainstorm with the instructor and a few class members. The group helps the actor decide what he or she could want from the other character that the inside person could not possibly anticipate. It helps if the outside character wants something of an emotional or a psychological nature rather than merely wanting physical goods. For instance, seeking comfort from the inside person has more potential than wanting to borrow twenty dollars.

    o The action may be based on previously shared information. If both actors agreed earlier, for example, that the inside character has a gambling problem, the outside character could demand that the inside person seek help now. The outside person cannot, however, change given circumstances having to do with the inside person. For instance, suddenly deciding that the inside character's parents were killed in a car wreck the previous week and basing an action on this newly created information is known as "playwriting." Rewriting a partner's history renders both actors unable to respond truthfully in the moment.

    o Once the actor decides what she or he wants from the partner, the actors play a silent improv. The outside actor attempts to get what she or he wants from the inside actor without miming or mouthing words, only through eye contact and physicality. When the improv has gone a certain distance, the instructor asks the actors to stop, let go of what just happened, and silently reset the scene. (Later in discussion, it is fascinating to learn how the inside person and the unknowing audience members have often understood very specifically what the outside person wants.)

- Play the same action adding language

  ○ The outside person goes offstage and, when he or she is ready, enters again to get what he or she wants from the inside character. (If the silent improv has been particularly intense, the onstage person can do some jumping jacks to shake off the moment and reset themselves. The offstage person can take as much time as they like before reentering.)

  ○ If either person would like to speak this time they may, but if there is nothing to say, it is best not to say anything.

  ○ With as few words as possible, the offstage actor (the initiator of action) attempts to get what she or he wants from the onstage actor (the receiver of action), who responds in the moment to what is happening. Although information established in the conversational setup of the relationship may come into play, excess verbiage of all kinds is discouraged. (Asking "why," going into long explanations, and exchanging pleasantries all get in the way of dynamic acting.)

## STEP #3: FURTHERING THE RELATIONSHIP

- Play a new improv with the positions reversed

  ○ The outside person becomes the inside person, and vice versa.

  ○ Decide at what point in time this new improv will occur in relation to the previous improv. (This can be two weeks later, six months later, or whatever seems best to the actors.)

  ○ If this is a new class session from Step 2, begin with a brief, silent improv where nothing is up to bring the relationship back into focus.

  ○ The outside actor meets with a group and decides: What just happened to the outside character that the inside character could not possibly know about and what (therefore) does the outside person want from their partner? This gives the outside person two tasks: (1) the preparation of a large experience they have just had, and (2) the pursuing of what they want from another person. (Creating the large event is a step that may be added at a later time. Sometimes the impact of the event is so large that it overwhelms the actor and dampens the urgency of pursuing the goal. On the other hand, doing both brings into sharp focus the actor's dilemma: big things are happening and yet one must *do* something.)

- o With as few words as possible, the new offstage actor attempts to get what she or he wants from the new inside person, who responds in the moment to what is happening.

## STEP #4: PREPARING A SCENE FROM *SPARE SCENES*

- Each pair selects or is assigned a scene from *Spare Scenes*

  - o Actors learn the lines by heart, forgoing particular line readings, meanings, and ideas about the words.

  - o In many scenes, there are indications that the pair is talking about something specific. Scene partners will need to decide whether to agree about what is being referred to ahead of time or to leave the topic open, so that one of the actors will make a specific decision privately, which will be a surprise to the other, in performance.

- Each pair decides the circumstances of the scene

  - o Actors decide where the scene is taking place, who will be in, who will be out, and when this scene is taking place in relation to the previous improvs the pair has done in Steps 2 and 3.

- The outside characters make choices

  - o Outside characters in the class can help each other brainstorm: what has just happened that the inside character could not possibly know about and what does the outside character want from the inside character that is of an unreasonable nature?

- The inside characters make choices

  - The inside characters, who are the receivers of action and don't have a pressing action to pursue from the outside characters, can also help each other decide their given circumstances. They may simply want to be hanging out in the agreed-upon space. Or the inside actor may want to select a physical activity to pursue. The physical activity should have a beginning, a middle, and an end, take at least five minutes to accomplish, and have some degree of difficulty in the doing of it. It helps if there is an emotional or a psychological reason why the activity needs to be accomplished right now. (Wrapping a present for an ill friend is a good physical activity; reading or doing aerobics are poorer choices.)

### STEP #5: PLAYING A SCENE FROM *SPARE SCENES*

- The actors play the scene

  - The outside character goes out to prepare while the inside character sets up and begins their physical activity.

  - The outside character enters and when the actor who has the first line feels the impulse to speak, she or he speaks the first line.

  - Each actor speaks their text, as memorized, in whatever way their partner and the circumstances of the scene are compelling them to speak.

  - The rate, inflection, tone, and delivery of the lines (all things that should not be a conscious concern of the actor) are completely dependent upon what is occurring between the actors in the moment. Although not attempting this for its own sake, the delivery of these lines will often be unexpected, fresh, startling, and visceral.

### STEP #6: PREPARING THE *SPARE SCENE* WITH THE POSITIONS REVERSED

- The outside person becomes the inside person, and vice versa

  - The partners decide when this new showing of the scene

will be taking place in relation to the previous showing in Step 5.

- ○ In some *Spare Scenes*, the initiator and receiver of the action are clearly delineated in the text, and switching acting roles may seem impossible. If this is the case, actors may try switching lines with one another, or using a new scene. It can be interesting, though, to keep the lines as they are, even if the words seem completely at odds with what is happening. When the initiator of action speaks what seems to be the receiver of action's lines and vice versa, what sense there is in the dialogue can be completely reversed in an interesting way. Other times, the tension between the words on the page and the action being played becomes too overpowering, and it is best to switch lines or scenes.

- The outside characters make choices

  - ○ Working as a group or individually, the outside characters choose something to want from the inside person. It is best if this new action is of a completely different nature than what the previous outside character wanted.

- The inside characters make choices

  - ○ Working as a group or individually, the inside characters determine a physical activity. It is best if this activity is of a completely different nature from what the previous inside character did.

## STEP #7: PLAYING THE SCENE WITH THE POSITIONS REVERSED

- The actors play the scene

  - ○ The outside person goes out to prepare while the inside character sets up and begins their physical activity.

  - ○ The outside character enters and when the actor who has the first line feels the impulse to speak, he or she speaks the first line.

  - ○ This second showing is often even more amazing because the characters, relationship, and lines are the same, but the scene will, of course, be completely different from the first time.

The entire process outlined above can be turned on its head in many ways. Rather than developing a relationship through conversation and improvisation, as outlined in Steps 1–3, actors can build a relationship through physical improvisation or any other method an acting class is exploring. Once a relationship is established, students can select for themselves a *Spare Scene* that speaks to the path they are developing. Or the text of a *Spare Scene* could be the starting point, with the actors developing characters, relationships, and circumstances inspired by the words on the page. In some scenes, physical business is implied and that might be the starting point upon which to build a scenario. However a scene is built, it is always valuable to play the *Spare Scene* a second time in a way that is somehow radically different from the first showing. Achieving this difference is accomplished by changing the action of one or both actors, adding potent circumstances, or a combination of the two.

# Exercises for the Directing Classroom

What a director actually does can be a difficult thing for new directors, actors, audiences, and even critics to determine. By keeping two variables constant—the actors and the words—the illusive role of the director can be illuminated through a variety of exercises with *Spare Scenes.*

## Step #1: The director builds a scene

- The director selects a scene from *Spare Scenes* and casts roles A and B

    ○ Actors learn lines by heart, forgoing particular line readings.

- The director and actors build a relationship between A and B

    ○ Directors can use relationship-building techniques listed in the acting exercises or those of their own choosing.

- The director sets up the given circumstances of the scene

    ○ Directors decide location of scene and which character is out and which is in.

    ○ Directors decide what the outside character wants from the inside character.

    ○ Directors decide what the inside character is doing.

## Step #2: The actors play the *Spare Scene*

    ○ The actors allow the given circumstances to impact their dialogue.

## STEP #3: THE DIRECTOR TACKLES THE CONCEPTUAL ISSUES OF THE SCENE

- What does the director want the audience to come away with after viewing the scene?

- How can the director achieve this result, using actor coaching, creation of environment, change of tone, pacing, or other theatrical elements?

## STEP #4: THE DIRECTOR COACHES THE ACTORS IN ORDER TO ILLUMINATE THE CONCEPT

- The director coaches the actors towards performances that illuminate the ideas the director wishes to highlight.

- In class, the instructor can side-coach the director as she or he is side-coaching the actors.

## STEP #3: THE DIRECTOR CREATES DIFFERENT ENVIRONMENTS

- Keeping all other variables the same (relationship, given circumstances, and intention), select a radically different environment in which the scene can take place.

- Environments can be created through the imagination only or with actual props, set pieces, and/or lighting.

- Directors can repeat this exercise, selecting a different locale for each new showing and directing the actors accordingly.

## STEP #4: THE DIRECTOR VARIES THE PACE

- Keeping all other variables the same, the director coaches the actors to play the scene at varying rates. (Using imagery to describe the pace to the actors can be helpful.)

## STEP #5: THE DIRECTOR ELICITS A DIFFERENT TONE

- Keeping all other variables the same, the director communicates to the actors a radically different tone in which to play the scene.

- Directors can repeat this exercise, selecting a different tone for each new showing. (It can be interesting to direct the

same scene in the manner of a suspenseful thriller, a slap-
stick farce, and a delicate drama.)

The process outlined above can be used in its entirety over the
course of several weeks or particular steps may be used as stand-
alone exercises. However *Spare Scenes* is utilized in the directing
classroom, it is valuable to direct a given scene in at least two different ways. With able actors, a director can direct the same words and
people in radically different directions. Because the skeletal language does not guide the actors in ways that traditional dialogue
can, the sometimes intangible director's work can be highlighted
more accurately.

# Short Scenes

# Short Scene 1

**A:** Hi.

**B:** Hey.

**A:** Whatcha doing.

**B:** Nothing.

**A:** Doesn't look like nothing.

**B:** That's what it is.

**A:** Can I do nothing too.

**B:** Up to you.

**A:** Doesn't sound inviting.

**B:** You need an invitation.

**A:** No.

**B:** What do you think you're doing.

**A:** Nothing.

**B:** I wouldn't call that nothing.

**A:** What would you call it.

**B:** I would call it something.

**A:** What would that something be.

**B:** I don't know.

**A:** Why not.

**B:** Look. What do you want?

**A:** Isn't that clear.

**B:** No.

**A:** Now is it.

# Short Scene 2

A: Are you up for this?

B: Why wouldn't I be.

A: You seem hesitant.

B: I'm not hesitant.

A: Okay.

B: You would like it if I was hesitant.

A: What.

B: Then you wouldn't have to do anything.

A: I want to.

B: That's what you say.

A: That's what I mean.

B: You're hoping I'll back out.

A: I'm worried you will.

B: I'm not.

A: Then everything's good.

B: Perfect.

A: What's up.

B: Nothing.

A: Right.

B: I said nothing.

A: Yeah right.

B: Now what.

A: Maybe . . .

# Short Scene 3

A: You got it.

B: I do.

A: You got it.

B: That's great.

A: Give me a little.

B: No way.

A: Just a little.

B: It's mine.

A: Come on.

B: Stay away.

A: Hey.

B: Back off.

A: You don't mean that.

B: I do.

A: You don't.

B: How do you know I don't.

A: Look at you.

B: What.

A: You've got it.

B: I do.

A: So share.

B: Why should I.

A: Lots of reasons.

# Short Scene 4

A: Take it easy.

B: Didn't see you there.

A: What's the rush.

B: Trying to get this done.

A: In record time.

B: No just want to get it done.

A: Conscientious.

B: No.

A: A fit of responsibility.

B: Wish it would rub off.

A: Okay.

B: There's plenty to do here.

A: Okay.

B: You can pitch in.

A: I don't think so.

B: Figured.

A: Why ask.

B: Hope springs eternal.

A: Quaint.

B: Wanting you to help?

A: The phrase.

B: I need to get this done.

A: No one's stopping you.

# Short Scene 5

A: What on earth.

B: I don't know.

A: What do you mean.

B: I don't know.

A: What's going on.

B: I don't know.

A: Give me a break.

B: I don't.

A: Guess.

B: I . . .

A: What.

B: I . . .

A: What is going on.

B: Not much.

A: You call this not much.

B: Well . . .

A: Okay that's it.

B: No.

A: I mean it this time.

B: Don't.

A: I will.

B: I'll change.

A: How.

# Short Scene 6

A: I do not.

B: You do too.

A: Do not.

B: You always do.

A: I never do.

B: You do without knowing it.

A: I do not.

B: Okay you don't.

A: I don't.

B: You do. I'm saying you don't.

A: What for.

B: To gain favor.

A: To gain favor.

B: Yes.

A: That's odd.

B: Not really.

A: It is.

B: People do it all the time.

A: No they don't.

B: I do.

A: With others.

B: Just you.

A: You sure.

# Short Scene 7

A: Whoa.

B: What.

A: That is too far.

B: Where.

A: You are over the edge.

B: How.

A: You've got to back off.

B: Why.

A: People will talk.

B: Who.

A: This is insane.

B: What.

A: You've pushed the limits.

B: Where.

A: You've pressed the buttons.

B: How.

A: You've got to lay off.

B: Why.

A: Because of what people will think.

B: Who.

A: Are you listening to me.

B: What.

A: Stop doing that now.

# Short Scene 8

A: What's going on?

B: Not much.

A: Not much.

B: Not much.

A: Doesn't look that way to me.

B: It doesn't.

A: No it doesn't.

B: Are you starting again.

A: Pardon.

B: You know what I mean.

A: I have no idea what you mean.

B: You're nuts.

A: Great.

B: Totally nuts.

A: Get off that.

B: Fine by me.

A: Oh. The silent treatment.

B: Say whatever you like.

A: You won't answer.

B: Why is everything difficult.

A: Difficult.

B: Is it possible to lighten up.

A: I'm not sure.

# Short Scene 9

A: Do you know what I think?

B: What.

A: This can all be worked out.

B: Really.

A: Easily.

B: What makes you sure.

A: Gut feeling.

B: That's reassuring.

A: It is, isn't it.

B: No it's not.

A: Why not.

B: It's not reassuring.

A: It'll work out.

B: Says your guts.

A: Says my guts.

B: I don't trust your guts.

A: Why.

B: Your guts are often wrong.

A: My guts are always right.

B: Your memory fails.

A: My memory and my guts are right.

B: An interesting thought.

A: A true thought.

# Short Scene 10

A: How about that.

B: Wow.

A: Double wow.

B: Triple wow.

A: You're weird.

B: You're weird.

A: I'm normal.

B: To a certain extent.

A: To a great extent.

B: Whatever.

A: It's exciting.

B: It is.

A: Unexpected.

B: I'll say.

A: Triple wow.

B: Yeah triple wow.

A: What do you really think.

B: Triple wow.

A: Triple wow.

B: Triple wow.

A: You've never said triple wow.

B: Not until now.

A: No . . .

# Short Scene 11

A: That is not right.

B: I know.

A: It's not right.

B: I know.

A: So why.

B: I don't know.

A: You know.

B: I don't.

A: You won't say.

B: I can't.

A: It's wrong.

B: I know.

A: So say something.

B: It's wrong.

A: Something new.

B: It's inevitable.

A: Inevitable.

B: Yes.

A: Not true.

B: It is.

A: Prove it.

B: Okay.

A: How.

# Short Scene 12

A: Are you scared.

B: Mostly.

A: Now.

B: Of course.

A: Why.

B: I'm always.

A: Always.

B: Always.

A: But sometimes.

B: Always.

A: Why.

B: Can't say.

A: Can't or won't.

B: Both.

A: Can't be.

B: It is.

A: You're unable or you refuse.

B: Both.

A: It's one or the other.

B: Sometimes it's both.

A: It can't be.

B: You scared.

A: I don't know.

# Short Scene 13

A: You have got to be kidding.

B: I am not kidding.

A: You have got to be.

B: Why would I.

A: It's impossible.

B: It's not impossible.

A: It's crazy.

B: No it's not.

A: Says who.

B: Says me and all sane people.

A: I wouldn't call you sane.

B: What would you call me?

A: Many things.

B: Such as.

A: You're avoiding the situation.

B: I'm willing to address the situation.

A: You're willing to be weird.

B: Such judgment.

A: I'm not judging. I'm . . .

B: You're . . .

A: I'm . . .

B: Is it difficult?

A: Sometimes.

# Short Scene 14

A: That's a switch.

B: A switch.

A: A real change.

B: Not a change.

A: A one-eighty.

B: Not really.

A: Complete reversal.

B: No way.

A: Absolutely.

B: Not really.

A: You can't deny it.

B: I can deny it.

A: You can but it's not true.

B: It is true.

A: Then you did change.

B: My denial is true.

A: Your denial is false.

B: Untrue.

A: Your change is true.

B: That's false.

A: You changed.

B: You've changed.

A: Now that's false.

# Short Scene 15

A: You want to be surprised.

B: Not really.

A: Come on. You want to be surprised.

B: I hate surprises.

A: You don't hate surprises.

B: I do. I hate them.

A: I never knew that.

B: Yes you did.

A: No I didn't.

B: I hate surprises.

A: This is different.

B: Okay.

A: You want to be surprised.

B: No.

A: Come on.

B: No.

A: Get with it.

B: I am with it.

A: Not really.

B: I am with it.

A: You are not with it.

B: I am.

A: This is not with it.

# Short Scene 16

A: Did you ever wonder.

B: Yes I have.

A: What did you think.

B: I was never sure.

A: It's not easy.

B: No it's not.

A: It's hard to know.

B: You got that right.

A: So many choices.

B: So little time.

A: Really.

B: It's hard.

A: No clear answers.

B: No help finding the answers.

A: I'll help you.

B: No.

A: I'll help you.

B: Right.

A: Of course.

B: I don't think.

A: Why not.

B: You'll help.

A: I said I would.

# Short Scene 17

A: Hello.

B: Hi.

A: It's been awhile.

B: It has.

A: Not long.

B: No.

A: But still.

B: Yes.

A: Long time.

B: You're the same.

A: I am.

B You are.

A: You've changed.

B: No.

A: You have.

B: Not true.

A: Yes.

B: You've changed.

A: You said . . .

B: You have.

A: Tell me.

B: Different.

A: Not true.

# Short Scene 18

A: What did you mean by that.

B: Nothing.

A: No really. What did you mean by that.

B: Nothing at all.

A: That wasn't nothing.

B: It was.

A: It wasn't.

B: It was.

A: If it was nothing, there wouldn't be anything to talk about.

B: There isn't.

A: We are.

B: What.

A: Talking about something.

B: Not really.

A: So there was something.

B: Hmmm.

A: What did you mean by that.

B: What are we talking about.

A: I think you know.

B: I'm completely lost.

A: Well that's true.

B: Is that what we're talking about.

A: We could, but that would be another topic.

# Short Scene 19

A: Do you believe me.

B: Yes mostly.

A: Mostly.

B: Yes mostly.

A: But not always.

B: Usually always.

A: Usually.

B: Yes usually.

A: But not absolutely always.

B: Guess not.

A: Why not.

B: I don't know.

A: That's strange.

B: Not really.

A: It is.

B: Why.

A: You know why.

B: I don't.

A: You should believe me always.

B: Nobody believes anyone always.

A: That's not true.

B: Of course it's true.

A: Cynical.

# Short Scene 20

A: You there?

B: I'm here.

A: Everything okay.

B: Yes.

A: Sure.

B: Yes.

A: You seem . . .

B: Yes.

A: Why.

B: Don't know.

A: Me.

B: No.

A: You're sure.

B: Yes.

A: I wonder.

B: Don't.

A: I can't help it.

B: You.

A: Yes.

B: I thought . . .

A: I know.

B: You.

A: Yes.

# Short Scene 21

A: Hi.

B: Hi.

A: This okay.

B: Great.

A: Really.

B: Of course.

A: Because . . .

B: It's fine.

A: Great.

B: And.

A: Nothing really.

B: Oh.

A: Just here.

B: I see.

A: No agenda.

B: Uh huh.

A: Carry on.

B: I will.

A: You sure.

B: Positive.

A: Need help.

B: Not sure.

A: Okay.

# Short Scene 22

A: You like that.

B: Yes. You.

A: It's okay.

B: Okay.

A: Yes. Okay.

B: Not great.

A: No not great.

B: But good.

A: Yes. Pretty good.

B: Pretty good.

A: Yes.

B: Wow.

A: What.

B: I had this wrong.

A: What.

B: I thought this was great.

A: Huh.

B: The greatest.

A: Well.

B: But now.

A: I said pretty good.

B: Sounds like no.

A: I never said no.

# Short Scene 23

A: I'm worried.

B: You aren't.

A: I am.

B: You can't.

A: I worry.

B: No need.

A: No need.

B: No way.

A: You avoid.

B: I don't.

A: I think.

B: You stew.

A: I consider.

B: You fret.

A: You fake.

B: Now that's . . .

A: I mean . . .

B: You.

A: I.

B: What.

A: I worry.

B: Anything else.

A: I . . .

# Short Scene 24

A: You mean it.

B: I do.

A: You do.

B: I do.

A: No question.

B: No question.

A: That's great.

B: I'm glad.

A: You're sure.

B: I am. You sure.

A: Me.

B: Yes you.

A: Of course.

B: I see.

A: Why ask.

B: I wonder.

A: About me.

B: I do.

A: You do.

B: I do.

A: How long.

B: Quite awhile.

A: You never said.

# Short Scene 25

A: What do you want.

B: I think you know.

A: I don't.

B: You do.

A: I don't.

B: You can guess.

A: Tell me.

B: Something.

A: What.

B: You know.

A: So say.

B: I have.

A: But now.

B: I want . . .

A: Yes.

B: I want . . .

A: I'm waiting.

B: You know.

A: So say.

B: I can't.

A: Try.

B: Okay.

A: I'm waiting.

# Short Scene 26

A: Hey.

B: Hi.

A: Wow.

B: Yeah.

A: Huh.

B: I know.

A: Never thought.

B: Neither did I.

A: Nice surprise.

B: I guess.

A: Don't you think.

B: Sure.

A: Unexpected is good.

B: It can be.

A: This is good.

B: I guess so.

A: You know so.

B: I do.

A: You know you do.

B: I do.

A: Of course.

B: Maybe.

A: Definitely.

# Short Scene 27

A: I wish.

B: What.

A: I wish.

B: What.

A: I don't know.

B: What.

A: I wish.

B: That's it.

A: Yes.

B: You wish.

A: Yes.

B: For.

A: I wish.

B: I see.

A: You don't.

B: I do.

A: Do you.

B: I do.

A: Really.

B: I do.

A: I do too.

B: You do.

A: I do.

# Short Scene 28

A: Hey.

B: What.

A: Nothing.

B: Why.

A: What.

B: What.

A: Nothing.

B: What.

A: Nothing.

B: What did you want.

A: Nothing.

B: You wanted something.

A: No.

B: You did.

A: I didn't.

B: You asked me.

A: I changed my mind.

B: You wanted something.

A: Sure.

B: What.

A: Nothing.

B: What was it.

A: Nothing now.

# Short Scene 29

A: Really.

B: I mean it.

A: Sure.

B: I am.

A: Okay.

B: Yes.

A: Yes.

B: Great.

A: So.

B: Yes.

A: Now.

B: Well.

A: Really.

B: Yes.

A: I . . .

B: Yes.

A: I'm not sure.

B: Try.

A: I want to.

B: Please.

A: Please.

B: Okay.

A: I think.

# Short Scene 30

A: Can you imagine.

B: Hard to picture.

A: Could it be.

B: I think it is.

A: Do you know.

B: I think I do.

A: With utter certainty.

B: I think so.

A: I wish I knew.

B: You know.

A: I don't.

B: Of course.

A: I don't.

B: You do.

A: You can't.

B: I do.

A: You know you don't.

B: I do.

A: You hope you know.

B: I know I know.

A: You wish.

B: I know.

A: You hope.

# Longer Scenes

# Scene 31

A: Where have you been?

B: Out and about.

A: Doing.

B: This and that.

A: What.

B: Nothing really.

A: If it's nothing, why not just say?

B: If it's nothing, there's nothing to say.

A: No one does nothing.

B: I do sometimes.

A: How do you do nothing.

B: Watch.

A: Very funny.

B: I can be amusing.

A: Sometimes.

B: Often.

A: Occasionally.

B: Regularly.

A: Periodically.

B: Dependably.

A: Where were you.

B: Out. Where were you.

A: In.

B: What were you doing?

A: Nothing.

B: Aha.

A: Reading.

B: Reading what?

A: Look what were you doing?

B: You have a suspicious mind.

A: No.

B: Just nosy?

A: I want to know.

B: What if I don't tell you.

A: There will be repercussions.

B: Sounds serious.

A: Is serious.

B: Why is everything serious with you?

A: Everything is not serious with me.

B: Seems so lately.

A: What do you mean lately.

B: Something's different.

A: With me.

B: With you.

A: Nothing's different with me.

B: Oh yes.

A: Name one thing.

B: You're suspicious.

A: Am not.

B: Are too. Why?

A: There are reasons.

B: There are no reasons.

A: Maybe I can't know for certain.

B: Maybe no one knows for certain.

# Scene 32

A: Do you believe that.

B: Unbelievable.

A: Crazy.

B: Weird.

A: Beyond weird.

B: Wild.

A: Totally wild.

B: What do you think.

A: I say we go for it.

B: No.

A: I say we go for it.

B: No way.

A: We just do it.

B: We can't.

A: We obviously can.

B: We can't.

A: Why not.

B: You know why not.

A: No I don't.

B: You do.

A: Why not.

B: It's wrong.

A: It's not wrong.

B: It's absolutely wrong.

A: It's not absolutely wrong.

B: Of course it is.

A: It's just this once.

B: Once or a million times, it's wrong.

A: Once is not wrong.

B: Of course it is.

A: Once is marginally wrong.

B: See.

A: Or marginally right.

B: Half full, half empty.

A: Right.

B: Wrong.

A: Right.

B: You can twist it your way.

A: I'm not twisting.

B: You have to twist to make it right.

A: I'm not twisting.

B: You are.

A: I'm not.

B: I'm not with you.

A: Yes you are.

B: No I'm not.

A: You're with me.

B: I'm not.

A: Deep down you are.

B: Deep down, on the surface, I'm not.

A: I know you.

B: I know you.

A: You're with me.

B: I'm not.

A: You're slipping.

# Scene 33

A: Wow. I am amazed.

B: Really. Do you like it.

A: Very cool.

B: I went all out.

A: I can tell.

B: Should I change this.

A: I wouldn't change a thing.

B: Seriously.

A: Seriously.

B: You mean it.

A: Of course.

B: You've never been this supportive.

A: I haven't.

B: Not really.

A: I'm always supportive.

B: In a vague way.

A: I'm not vaguely supportive.

B: Yes. Vaguely supportive.

A: I'm tremendously supportive.

B: That's what you think.

A: It's the truth.

B: Our versions of the truth differ.

A: Where is this coming from?

B: You're oblivious.

A: I'm not.

B: You don't see what's under your nose.

A: What are you talking about.

B: I think it's best if you figure it out.

A: What if I can't come up with anything.

B: Stay in oblivion.

A: Oblivion.

B: Yeah.

A: I'm in oblivion.

B: Looks that way to me.

A: You have that wrong.

B: I don't and you know it.

A: I know everything about you.

B: Yeah.

A: I know exactly what you're thinking.

B: That would amaze me.

A: I know your ups and downs.

B: Really.

A: I've been through it all with you.

B: You've been an observer.

A: I know a lot more than you think.

B: Such as.

A: You'll find out.

B: What's that supposed to mean.

A: You'll see.

B: Is this a game.

A: Maybe you're in oblivion.

# Scene 34

A: What are you doing here?

B: I have a right.

A: What are you doing?

B: What do you care.

A: Explain yourself.

B: That would be difficult.

A: Yes it would, but do it.

B: And if I say no.

A: I'll kick you out.

B: I don't think you can.

A: I think I can.

B: Interesting.

A: Not really.

B: Very interesting.

A: Just get out.

B: Why should I.

A: Because I said so.

B: Ah because you said so.

A: Yes.

B: Another interesting thought.

A: Not really. Get out.

B: Do you really want me to go?

A: Believe it or not I do.

B: But we could have so much fun.

A: Doing.

B: Old times.

A: Old times sucked.

B: Old times were great.

A: Old times were twisted.

B: Not true.

A: I'm beyond that.

B: Oooh.

A: Way beyond.

B: Ouch.

A: So move along.

B: You don't mean it.

A: I do.

B: You haven't asked me about me.

A: How are you.

B: Fine thanks.

A: Great. Get out.

B: Just like that.

A: Just like that.

B: There's so much you don't know.

A: Yeah.

B: A lot you don't understand.

A: That's tough to believe.

B: Give me a minute.

A: You've had more than a minute.

B: I can change your mind.

A: Impossible.

B: Nothing's impossible.

A: Some things are.

B: Not this.

A: You'll see.

# Scene 35

A: I've always liked that.

B: Me too.

A: Always thought that was great.

B: Me too.

A: Seems dumb now.

B: Yeah.

A: Childish.

B: In a way.

A: Ever wish you didn't have to grow up.

B: Yep.

A: Avoid the whole adult thing.

B: The issues.

A: The heartaches.

B: It's not that bad.

A: I'm not sure.

B: Depends on how you look at it.

A: I guess so.

B: Hey come on.

A: No you're right.

B: It's not that bad.

A: I guess not.

B: I thought you were different.

A: Really.

B: Strong.

A: Strong.

B: A rock.

A: No way.

B: You are.

A: People think.

B: You are.

A: If you knew.

B: I do know.

A: You know jack.

B: I know lots.

A: I wish you did.

B: I do.

A: I wish . . .

B: What.

A: Nothing.

B: Tell me.

A: It doesn't matter.

B: It does.

A: Wishes are . . .

B: Important.

A: Irrelevant.

B: No.

A: Unreasonable.

B: Reason is overrated.

A: Reason gets you up in the morning.

B: Many things get you up in the morning.

A: I wonder.

B: Tell me.

A: I wish I could.

# Scene 36

A: Always thinking aren't you?

B: Something's always ticking.

A: Always on top of things.

B: It's all right here.

A: Must be nice.

B: 'Tis, 'tis.

A: Never worried about a wrong move.

B: No.

A: Always well thought out.

B: Yes.

A: You sure.

B: What's up.

A: You're in for a surprise.

B: I doubt that.

A: I think so.

B: On the contrary.

A: Yes.

B: I think you might be surprised.

A: Not me.

B: Yes.

A: Not this time.

B: 'Fraid so.

A: You'd love that.

B: I wouldn't.

A: You'd act like you wouldn't but you would.

B: I wouldn't want you to be caught off guard.

A: Don't worry. Not a problem.

B: I think it might be.

A: It's not. I've got it under control.

B: All right up there.

A: Learned it from you.

B: Is that right.

A: Yes.

B: I'm flattered.

A: Well.

B: You're like me.

A: Not exactly.

B: Then.

A: Learned some things from you.

B: I see.

A: Things to get me by.

B: Such as.

A: This and that.

B: Right.

A: You'll be surprised.

B: I doubt that.

A: Oh I think you will.

B: No way.

A: Watch your back.

B: Because.

A: Watch your back is all.

B: I don't believe . . .

A: You never know.

# Scene 37

A: Hey.

B: Cut that out.

A: Come on.

B: Cut it out.

A: Grow up.

B: You grow up.

A: What's up.

B: Not much.

A: Hey.

B: Lay off.

A: Come on.

B: Lay off.

A: What's wrong.

B: I'm trying to concentrate.

A: Stand back.

B: Is anything serious with you.

A: Absolutely not.

B: Didn't think so.

A: Of course.

B: I never see that side.

A: What is up.

B: I'm trying to concentrate.

A: So concentrate.

B: It's difficult.

A: Ignore me.

B: Right.

A: Ignore me.

B: Lay off.

A: No.

B: Grow up.

A: Never.

B: Get out of my life.

A: That hurts.

B: Get out.

A: You get out.

B: I was here first.

A: And.

B: Grow up.

A: Lighten up.

B: Will you ever change.

A: Why.

B: People move on.

A: I'm not moving on.

B: People grow.

A: I'm done growing.

B: You haven't started.

A: You have.

B: I'm trying.

A: Look at you.

B: I need to move on.

A: So move on.

B: I am.

A: You're too good for me.

B: I didn't say that.

# Scene 38

A: You are something else.

B: Thanks.

A: I mean it.

B: Thank you. That's sweet.

A: No thank you.

B: You're welcome.

A: Gotta go.

B: So soon.

A: Have to.

B: Hey.

A: Yes.

B: Nothing.

A: No what.

B: You've gotta go.

A: I can stay.

B: Don't want to keep you.

A: You're not keeping me. What.

B: Ever wonder . . .

A: Yes.

B: About the crazy turns in life.

A: Yes.

B: About how things end up.

A: Yes.

B: Could go one way, could go another.

A: Yes.

B: Life could be different.

A: Oh.

B: Oh no.

A: No it's fine.

B: I meant.

A: It's fine.

B: It's not.

A: I should go.

B: I'm sorry.

A: You didn't say anything.

B: You know.

A: It's fine.

B: Fine.

A: Fine is good.

B: Distant.

A: Close.

B: You know what I mean.

A: I'm not sure.

B: I'm not either.

A: This is unexpected.

B: We could try.

A: That scares me.

B: Slowly.

A: But.

B: Or not.

A: Wait.

B: Yes.

A: Maybe.

B: Really.

A: Maybe.

B: This is unexpected.

# Scene 39

A: What do you want.

B: I don't know.

A: Anything. What do you want.

B: I don't know. You decide.

A: I always decide.

B: I have no preference.

A: You say that.

B: I mean that.

A: You know that's not true.

B: Of course it is.

A: No one thinks that way.

B: I do.

A: No one always defers.

B: I have no preference.

A: You do. You can't admit it.

B: I would admit it if I did.

A: You're blocked.

B: I'm not blocked.

A: You're blocked like an artery.

B: I'm not blocked like an artery.

A: You're a heart attack waiting to happen.

B: What are you talking about.

A: A walking angioplasty.

B: What.

A: An analogy.

B: I'm not blocked.

A: You are.

B: I'm done.

A: You can't face your own limitations.

B: I'm not limited.

A: You can't make a decision.

B: I make thousands everyday.

A: You don't.

B: I do.

A: You never do.

B: Of course I do.

A: Not in front of me.

B: If it doesn't happen in front of you it doesn't happen.

A: I've never seen it.

B: Trust me.

A: Prove it.

B: I don't need to prove it.

A: Prove it.

B: Not necessary.

A: Prove me wrong.

B: That would be easy.

A: So do something easy.

B: I prefer slow torture.

A: You do this on purpose.

B: A way to pass the time.

A: You don't make decisions on purpose.

B: I don't know.

A: You do this to torture me.

B: I don't know.

# Scene 40

A: It's settled.

B: It's settled.

A: Absolutely.

B: No way.

A: It is.

B: You're kidding.

A: I'm not.

B: You're serious.

A: I am.

B: You're a genius.

A: Not really.

B: You are.

A: Okay I am.

B: You're amazing.

A: That's true.

B: Nearly flawless.

A: Nearly.

B: No one's perfect.

A: Some come close.

B: And you're in that club.

A: Of course.

B: Of course.

A: Of course.

B: Mighty sure of yourself.

A: Who wouldn't be.

B: I wouldn't be.

A: That's you.

B: No I mean if I were you.

A: If you were me you wouldn't be?

B: Right.

A: Ha.

B: That's right.

A: Ha. Ha.

B: Funny.

A: Very.

B: Not really.

A: I can laugh.

B: If that helps.

A: Helps.

B: Ease the pain.

A: I'm not in pain.

B: Denial is a form of pain.

A: I'm not in denial plus denial's not painful.

B: It's the worst pain.

A: But you don't feel it if you're in denial.

B: Exactly.

A: You're one to mention denial.

B: You're one to mention perfection.

A: I only mention what's true.

B: Or what you'd like to be true.

A: What's your version of true.

B: Depends on who's asking.

A: That's me asking.

B: I'd answer but I'm in denial.

A: In pain too.

B: I can't tell.

# Scene 41

A: That is hilarious.

B: Very funny.

A: It is.

B: I know.

A: You know.

B: I know.

A: Then why do you . . .

B: Why do I what.

A: Act that way.

B: What way.

A: You know what way.

B: I do not act that way.

A: Then you don't know what I'm talking about.

B: I do and I don't.

A: Yes you do.

B: No I don't.

A: Of course you do.

B: I absolutely don't. But you do.

A: Now that is rich.

B: Rich.

A: Yes rich.

B: Caloric.

A: Is that a word.

B: Yes. Three syllables.

A: Like I don't use three syllable words.

B: I did not say that.

A: You intimated that.

B: Four syllables. Very good.

A: There you go again.

B: I was congratulating you.

A: You were slamming me.

B: Saying four syllables is a slam.

A: Your intonation.

B: Another four syllables.

A: Oh stop.

B: Back to one.

A: Is this worth continuing.

B: I don't know, is it.

A: Depends on what you mean.

B: What do you mean.

A: I don't know if I can come up with the right words.

B: You can.

A: The syllable police are listening.

B: They've gone away.

A: Sure.

B: Sure.

A: Can this work.

B: Can it.

A: Depends on commitment.

B: Three syllables.

A: At least.

# Scene 42

A: Hey.

B: Miss you.

A: You do.

B: Of course.

A: Really.

B: Why not.

A: Just surprised.

B: Why surprised.

A: Didn't think . . .

B: Of course.

A: Really.

B: I miss you.

A: That's kind.

B: Not kind.

A: Not kind.

B: I miss you.

A: That's kind.

B: No. Miss you.

A: Not kind.

B: Not kind.

A: What then.

B: Deeply.

A: Deeply.

B: Yes.

A: That's not kind.

B: No.

A: That's . . .

B: More.

A: Oh.

B: Kind is . . .

A: Surface.

B: Yes.

A: I miss you.

B: That's . . .

A: Deep.

B: It is.

A: Absolutely.

B: You do.

A: I do.

B: But you never . . .

A: You never . . .

B: I didn't think.

A: You should have asked.

B: I didn't think.

A: Too late now.

B: Too late.

A: Of course it is.

B: But . . .

A: Can't be otherwise.

B: But . . .

A: Have to be kind.

B: Kind is . . .

A: Surface.

B: Yes.

A: Surface it is.

B: But . . .

# Scene 43

A: Wow. You are terrific.

B: Thanks.

A: I mean it. Really great.

B: Thanks.

A: How did you get to be you.

B: Just happened.

A: I wish I could be more like you.

B: That would be boring.

A: No really.

B: We'd bore each other.

A: I think it would be fun.

B: I like you as you are.

A: Really.

B: Absolutely.

A: Wouldn't change a thing.

B: Well.

A: Yes.

B: Kidding.

A: Funny.

B: Maybe . . .

A: What.

B: A sliver of change.

A: How.

B: Here and there.

A: What's that mean.

B: Little changes to a masterpiece.

A: Masterpieces don't need changing.

B: Sometimes.

A: That's what makes them a masterpiece.

B: Okay. So I wouldn't change anything.

A: But you said.

B: I was being picky.

A: So be picky.

B: Not worth it.

A: You started. Be picky.

B: Okay.

A: Yes.

B: The way you drive at things.

A: What way.

B: The way you can't let go.

A: I'm easygoing.

B: You hang on like a terrier.

A: I release. I always release.

B: You clamp down.

A: I move on.

B: Rarely.

A: I always let go.

B: Not in my experience.

A: It must be you then.

B: Maybe.

A: Everyone else thinks I'm carefree.

B: Interesting.

A: Everyone else thinks I'm terrific. Really great.

B: Okay.

A: That's it. Okay.

# Scene 44

A: Get out.

B: I mean it.

A: Get out.

B: It's true.

A: Get out.

B: I'm not kidding.

A: That's fantastic.

B: What did I tell you.

A: You're sure.

B: Positive.

A: For real.

B: Absolutely.

A: This is great.

B: Really great.

A: This means the world.

B: Don't I know.

A: You're positive.

B: I am.

A: Wow.

B: Happy.

A: Happy.

B: Happy.

A: Doesn't begin to describe it.

B: What's it like.

A: Walking on the moon.

B: Wow.

A: Sailing through the universe.

B: Awesome.

A: Seeing God.

B: Really.

A: Yes. I see God.

B: What's He look like.

A: Metaphorically.

B: Oh.

A: He's a feeling. Not a face.

B: Right.

A: An all-encompassing feeling of well-being.

B: Yes.

A: Everything's taken care of.

B: Yes.

A: From here on it's smooth sailing.

B: You think.

A: I know.

B: You're sure.

A: I'm positive.

B: Hmmm.

A: What.

B: I'm not sure.

A: Why.

B: I wouldn't be too sure.

A: I am.

B: Watch it.

A: Watch it.

B: I'd watch it.

A: What do you know.

B: I'd watch it.

# Scene 45

A: I've always loved days like this.

B: You've got to be kidding.

A: Invigorating.

B: Debilitating.

A: That's a narrow view.

B: A realistic view.

A: Realism is overrated.

B: Rosy-colored glasses are overrated.

A: All of life is overrated.

B: Exactly.

A: Let's give up.

B: Sounds good.

A: That's pathetic.

B: Realistic.

A: What is this realism kick.

B: It's the way I lead my life.

A: Don't I know.

B: Seem to have forgotten.

A: How could I.

B: I'm not sure but you did.

A: There are so many possibilities.

B: Not in this case.

A: Even in this case.

B: We're locked in.

A: Locked in.

B: Unable to move.

A: That's ridiculous.

B: What are our options.

A: We're free people.

B: We're trapped.

A: Trapped in your mind.

B: In my mind, in this situation, whatever.

A: Step outside.

B: Can't.

A: Step outside.

B: I wish we could.

A: We can.

B: We can't.

A: Well I can.

B: Go for it.

A: I will.

B: I'll see you back in a few.

A: If I choose to.

B: Even if you don't, I'll see you back.

A: Like all this is predetermined.

B: It is.

A: It isn't.

B: Believe what you want.

A: I will.

B: Because it doesn't really matter.

A: Of course it matters. It matters deeply.

B: You'll find out.

A: Life is good.

B: You'll find out.

# Scene 46

A: What do you want.

B: I told you.

A: What do you really want.

B: You know.

A: I don't. I'm asking.

B: I've told you.

A: Tell me again.

B: You don't remember.

A: Tell me.

B: I don't want anything.

A: You're content.

B: Yes.

A: With everything.

B: Yes.

A: No needs whatsoever.

B: None.

A: You just want to go along.

B: That's fine.

A: That's not fine.

B: Not fine.

A: I want more.

B: You.

A: I want more.

B: I don't believe you.

A: Why not.

B: You never want more.

A: I do now.

B: You always want less.

A: I've changed.

B: You're sure.

A: I'm sure.

B: So what do you want.

A: I want more.

B: How much more.

A: I want a lot.

B: Really.

A: Really.

B: A lot.

A: A whole lot.

B: I'm floored.

A: I'm ready.

B: I'm not.

A: You're not.

B: I'm not.

A: You always want more.

B: I've changed.

A: You've changed.

B: I have.

A: Since when.

B: Just now.

A: But why.

B: You've changed.

A: But when.

B: Just now.

# Scene 47

A: Come here.

B: No way.

A: Come here.

B: Why should I.

A: Because I'm asking nicely.

B: Says who.

A: Says me.

B: I don't call that nice.

A: What do you call it.

B: Your usual.

A: My usual.

B: Yes. Your usual.

A: What's my usual.

B: That way you have.

A: What way.

B: That way.

A: Oh. That way.

B: Yes. That way.

A: What are you talking about.

B: That way you have.

A: You like that way I have.

B: I pretend I like that way you have.

A: You pretend.

B: Yes. I pretend.

A: You don't pretend with me.

B: How do you know.

A: You don't.

B: Maybe I do.

A: I'm betting you don't.

B: What if I were pretending now.

A: I know what you're doing.

B: At all times.

A: At all times.

B: Maybe I do like your way.

A: I knew it.

B: Maybe I love your way.

A: That's clear.

B: Maybe I'm testing you.

A: Well drop that.

B: Or maybe I don't like your way.

A: You do.

B: Maybe I'd like another way.

A: What other way.

B: Just some other way.

A: With somebody else.

B: Maybe.

A: What do you mean maybe.

B: You've never thought.

A: Never.

B: Another way.

A: No.

B: Just this way.

A: Only this way.

B: Only this way.

# Scene 48

A: I've always loved that.

B: Really.

A: Always.

B: Honestly.

A: Always loved that.

B: Not me.

A: I know.

B: I don't like that.

A: I know.

B: How do you know.

A: I know you.

B: Well.

A: Deeply.

B: Really.

A: Truly.

B: And still.

A: I know.

B: We're different.

A: We are.

B: Our values.

A: Different.

B: That's tough.

A: Not insurmountable.

B: Says who.

A: Me.

B: You think.

A: I know.

B: What makes you certain.

A: I know.

B: I don't.

A: I know.

B: You know that too.

A: Yes.

B: You know a lot.

A: I do.

B: How come.

A: I'm sensitive.

B: Sensitive.

A: Yes.

B: To others.

A: Yes to others.

B: All others.

A: Some others.

B: How many others.

A: Don't know.

B: How many.

A: Not many.

B: A handful or three dozen.

A: Don't know.

B: To me.

A: To you.

B: You're sure.

A: I'm positive.

B: I'm not.

A: I know.

# Scene 49

A: Hi.

B: Hi there.

A: What's up.

B: Not much.

A: Everything okay.

B: Everything's great.

A: All in order.

B: All's well.

A: Who would have thought.

B: Who knew.

A: You sure.

B: Really. Things are fine.

A: I don't believe you.

B: You should.

A: I don't.

B: That's your choice.

A: Can you tell me the truth for once.

B: This is the truth.

A: I don't believe you.

B: That's your choice.

A: Quit saying that.

B: Okay.

A: Level with me.

B: I am.

A: Don't shut me out.

B: I'm not.

A: There's more here.

B: There's not.

A: So let's go then.

B: I'm not up for it.

A: Aha.

B: I'm not up for it.

A: Why not.

B: Not interested.

A: What's the real reason.

B: That's the real reason.

A: This is tiresome.

B: Definitely. Why don't you go.

A: Not without you.

B: That's ridiculous.

A: You're ridiculous.

B: I just want to stay here.

A: Why don't you trust me.

B: I do trust you.

A: Tell me the truth then.

B: There's nothing to tell.

A: There's plenty to tell. You choose not to.

B: Have it your way.

A: I wish I could.

B: You always do.

A: I never do.

B: That's not how I see it.

A: That's how everyone sees it.

B: Everyone.

A: Yes.

# Scene 50

A: Nice day.

B: Not really.

A: It is.

B: No it's not.

A: It's a nice day.

B: It's a lousy day.

A: It's a phrase.

B: So don't use it.

A: A phrase to get you through.

B: It's not accurate.

A: It's not meant to be accurate.

B: Don't use it if it's not accurate.

A: People say inaccurate things all the time.

B: I don't.

A: That's inaccurate.

B: No it isn't.

A: Of course it is.

B: I tell it like it is.

A: All the time.

B: That's right.

A: That's not the way I see it.

B: Well you're inaccurate.

A: Why does it revolve around you.

B: What.

A: Why does the world rotate around you.

B: Never thought about it that way.

A: You always think about it that way.

B: I never have.

A: You have without knowing.

B: The world goes on without me.

A: As will I.

B: It's a nice day.

A: Have a nice day.

B: Oh no you don't.

A: Oh yes I do.

B: Stay.

A: Why.

B: I'm asking.

A: So.

B: So stay.

A: Why should I.

B: It'll be fun.

A: Fun.

B: Yes, it's a nice day.

A: It is.

B: A lovely day.

A: No it's not.

B: I've changed my mind.

A: So have I.

B: Change it back.

A: Why should I.

B: Because it is a lovely day.

A: It's a nice day.

B: It's a nice day.

A: We'll see.

B: We'll see.

# Scene 51

A: Okay.

B: Yes.

A: Here's the thing.

B: Yes.

A: You and I.

B: You and me.

A: Whatever.

B: Yes.

A: Here's the thing.

B: I'm waiting.

A: Now that's the thing.

B: What.

A: That type of thing.

B: Which thing.

A: The thing you do.

B: What thing.

A: I'm waiting.

B: You're waiting.

A: No you said I'm waiting.

B: I was.

A: But the point is.

B: What is the point.

A: The point is you don't say that.

B: I did.

A: I know but you shouldn't.

B: Why can't I say that.

A: Because.

B: Now that is the thing.

A: What.

B: That is the thing I'm talking about.

A: You're not talking about anything.

B: I am now.

A: What thing.

B: I shouldn't.

A: Shouldn't what.

B: That's what you said.

A: There's nothing wrong with that.

B: There is everything wrong with that.

A: You're avoiding.

B: You're avoiding.

A: You're game playing.

B: You tell me I shouldn't.

A: Shouldn't game play.

B: Shouldn't anything.

A: I do not.

B: You just did.

A: But you shouldn't have.

B: Why not.

A: Because I had the floor.

B: You had the floor.

A: For once.

B: You always have the floor.

A: Not this floor.

# Scene 52

A: Isn't that lovely.

B: Lovely.

A: No really.

B: Really.

A: Lovely.

B: Lovely.

A: Come on.

B: What.

A: It's lovely.

B: I said that.

A: Did you mean it.

B: Of course.

A: Really.

B: No.

A: See.

B: Well.

A: I knew it.

B: So.

A: You're transparent.

B: A crime.

A: An observation.

B: What's wrong with being transparent.

A: No room for mystery.

B: I don't want to be mysterious.

A: Don't worry.

B: I'm happy in my transparency.

A: I know.

B: Transparency is good.

A: Saran wrap.

B: See.

A: Eyeglasses.

B: There you go.

A: Ice cubes.

B: All good things.

A: In their way.

B: Boring.

A: I didn't say that.

B: But.

A: Well.

B: You'd rather thick wool.

A: Sure.

B: Murky water.

A: That's it.

B: Dense fog.

A: You got it.

B: Mysterious.

A: Something more there.

B: As though that were better.

A: More substantial.

B: Or more fraught.

A: More depth.

B: More complication.

A: Okay.

B: Is this clear.

# Scene 53

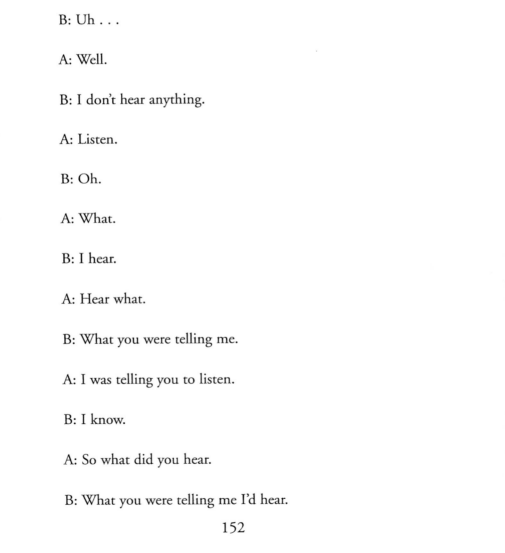

A: Listen.

B: Yes.

A: Listen.

B: Uh . . .

A: Well.

B: I don't hear anything.

A: Listen.

B: Oh.

A: What.

B: I hear.

A: Hear what.

B: What you were telling me.

A: I was telling you to listen.

B: I know.

A: So what did you hear.

B: What you were telling me I'd hear.

A: I was telling you to listen.

B: Okay.

A: Listen.

B: Okay.

A: Listening.

B: Yes.

A: All right then.

B: All right what.

A: Now you're listening.

B: I'm trying.

A: Before you said you heard.

B: Yes.

A: When you really didn't.

B: I was listening.

A: But you said you heard something.

B: I thought I did.

A: You lied.

B: I did not lie.

A: Of course you did. There was nothing to hear.

B: It was a trick question.

A: It was a simple request.

B: I was listening.

A: Hearing things that never made a sound.

B: I wanted to listen so much I actually heard something.

A: You wanted to jump to the result.

B: What.

A: You wanted to have heard something.

B: So.

A: Instead of just listening.

B: I was listening.

A: You were already on to the next thing.

B: I wasn't.

A: I wanted you to listen.

B: I know.

A: Listen.

B: Okay.

A: Can you.

# Scene 54

A: Hello.

B: Salutations.

A: Salutations.

B: Greetings.

A: Greetings.

B: Guess what.

A: What.

B: No guess.

A: I can't.

B: Try.

A: Tell me.

B: That's no fun.

A: It is.

B: It's not.

A: Try.

B: You . . .

A: No.

B: You . . .

A: No.

B: You . . .

A: No.

B: I give up.

A: Guess.

B: I tried.

A: Try again.

B: I can't.

A: Okay.

B: Wait.

A: What.

B: Tell me.

A: You gave up.

B: So.

A: So you're not interested.

B: I'm vitally interested.

A: Then guess.

B: No.

A: Okay.

B: Wait.

A: What.

B: Tell me.

A: You won't guess.

B: I won't.

A: So no.

B: What if.

A: What.

B: Nothing.

A: What.

B: Nothing.

A: Tell me.

B: Guess.

A: I can't.

B: Okay.

A: Wait.

# Scene 55

A: Hey.

B: Hi.

A: How goes it.

B: Okay.

A: Good.

B: You.

A: Fine.

B: Good.

A: Busy.

B: Yes.

A: Oh.

B: Why.

A: Nothing.

B: Why.

A: Need help.

B: What's wrong.

A: The usual.

B: You're kidding.

A: I'm not.

B: Again.

A: Again.

B: Just leave.

A: Leave.

B: Go.

A: I can't.

B: You can.

A: You know I can't.

B: You're weak.

A: I am.

B: So weak.

A: I am.

B: Why.

A: It's hard.

B: It's not that hard.

A: Of course it is.

B: It's not.

A: You don't understand.

B: You're right. I don't.

A: You could if you wanted to.

B: I want to.

A: No you don't.

B: I do. You don't let me.

A: I'm asking.

B: Too late.

A: Not too late.

B: Always too late.

A: That's not true.

B: So I can't help.

A: You could if you wanted.

B: I do.

A: I would never take time to say that.

B: Never.

A: Never.

B: Interesting.

A: Thank you.

# Scene 57

A: Okay.

B: Really.

A: Okay.

B: Great.

A: I guess.

B: You guess.

A: I guess.

B: Not sure.

A: I'm sure.

B: You guess.

A: I guess I'm sure.

B: That's lame.

A: I'm sure.

B: You're not.

A: I am.

B: You think.

A: I know.

B: What changed.

A: Nothing.

B: You guessed.

A: I'm sure.

B: You changed.

A: I'm sure.

B: I can't trust you.

A: You can.

B: I can't.

A: You don't want to.

B: I do.

A: You don't.

B: I do.

A: You never have.

B: I always have.

A: Why don't I know that.

B: You choose not to see.

A: See what's not there.

B: It's there.

A: It's not.

B: You want it not to be there.

A: Not true.

B: You hope it's not there.

A: That's not true.

B: You know it is.

A: Trust me.

B: Why should I.

A: Trust me.

B: Because.

A: Just do it.

B: I can't.

A: You won't.

B: I want to.

A: You do.

B: I do.

A: So do.

B: I can't.

A: Just try.

# Scene 58

A: Hello.

B: Hello.

A: Hello.

B: Hi.

A: Wow.

B: Yeah.

A: That's something.

B: It is.

A: Okay.

B: Okay.

A: Let's go.

B: Not so fast.

A: Why not.

B: Not so fast.

A: Let's go.

B: Later.

A: Later.

B: Later.

A: Not now.

B: Not now.

A: But why.

B: Why.

A: Yes why

B: You know why.

A: I do.

B: Come on.

A: I do.

B: You know.

A: I don't.

B: Then guess.

A: Uh . . .

B: Give up.

A: Give up.

B: I'm not telling.

A: Come on.

B: I'm not.

A: Just say.

B: Guess.

A: I can't.

B: You won't.

A: I can't.

B: You should.

A: I'll try.

B: So try.

A: You want to stay.

B: I know.

A: I guessed.

B: But why.

A: You . . .

B: Yes.

A: You . . .

B: Yes.

A: Really.

B: Yes.

# Scene 59

A: I want.

B: What.

A: I want.

B: What.

A: So much.

B: What.

A: Too much.

B: How.

A: I feel.

B: What.

A: I feel.

B: What.

A: So much.

B: What.

A: Too much.

B: So say.

A: Can't.

B: Just say.

A: Too hard.

B: Tell me.

A: Not you.

B: Why not.

A: Can't.

B: Of course you can.

A: Of course.

B: What.

A: You know.

B: I don't.

A: You know.

B: Okay.

A: Well.

B: Tell me.

A: You know.

B: I know.

A: So.

B: What.

A: What now.

B: I don't know.

A: See.

B: Yes.

A: What now.

B: Let's think.

A: I've tried.

B: Think together.

A: Okay.

B: Okay.

A: So.

B: I . . .

A: Yes.

B: I . . .

A: See.

B: Yes.

A: It's . . .

B: I know.

# Scene 60

A: You there?

B: I'm here.

A: Just wondering.

B: I'm here.

A: You okay.

B: I'm okay.

A: Just wondering.

B: I'm okay.

A: Whatcha doing.

B: Not much.

A: Not much.

B: Not much.

A: Just wondering.

B: Okay.

A: Any plans.

B: Not really.

A: You're sure.

B: Yeah sure.

A: Any thoughts.

B: Any thoughts.

A: Anything new.

B: Nothing new.

A: Seen anything lately.

B: Not really.

A: Nothing good.

B: No nothing.

A: Happy though.

B: Yes happy.

A: Content.

B: Content.

A: Searching.

B: Seeking.

A: Seeking.

B: As always.

A: But nothing new.

B: No nothing new.

A: Seeking.

B: Yes seeking.

A: But content.

B: Mildly.

A: Mildly.

B: Yes mildly.

A: Not completely.

B: Not completely.

A: What's missing.

B: Missing.

A: Missing.

B: Don't know.

A: Don't know.

B: Just seeking.

A: Something . . .

B: Unknown.

A: Unknown.

B: Out there.

A: Not here.

B: Maybe.